Put Beginning Readers on the Right Track with
ALL ABOARD READING™

The All Aboard Reading series is especially for beginning readers. Written by noted authors and illustrated in full color, these are books that children really and truly *want* to read—books to excite their imagination, tickle their funny bone, expand their interests, and support their feelings. With four different reading levels, All Aboard Reading lets you choose which books are most appropriate for your children and their growing abilities.

Picture Readers—for Ages 3 to 6
Picture Readers have super-simple texts, with many nouns appearing as rebus pictures. At the end of each book are 24 flash cards—on one side is the rebus picture; on the other side is the written-out word.

Level 1—for Preschool through First-Grade Children
Level 1 books have very few lines per page, very large type, easy words, lots of repetition, and pictures with visual "cues" to help children figure out the words on the page.

Level 2—for First-Grade to Third-Grade Children
Level 2 books are printed in slightly smaller type than Level 1 books. The stories are more complex, but there is still lots of repetition in the text, and many pictures. The sentences are quite simple and are broken up into short lines to make reading easier.

Level 3—for Second-Grade through Third-Grade Children
Level 3 books have considerably longer texts, harder words, and more complicated sentences.

All Aboard for happy reading!

For Mom and Dad, who taught me to read—D.B.

Photo Credits: front cover, Jed Jacobsohn / Allsport; back cover spot, Tom Hauck / Allsport; p. 1, Tom Hauck / Allsport, p. 2, Tom Hauck / Allsport; p. 3, Todd Warshaw / Allsport; chapter opener spots, Al Bello / Allsport; p. 5, Robert Laberge / Allsport; p. 8, AFP / Corbis; p 10. Allsport; p. 11, Jim Gund / Allsport; p. 14, From the collection of the Texas Hall of Fame, Waco, TX; p. 16, Bob Daemrich / Allsport; p. 18, Brad Messina / Allsport; p. 19, Anton Want / Allsport; p. 21, Lou Capazzola, p. 23, Jonathan Daniel / Allsport; p. 24-25, Tom Hauck; p. 27, Doug Pensinger / Allsport; p. 29; Tom Hauck / Allsport; p. 31, Tom Hauck / Allsport; p. 33; Tom Hauck / Allsport; p. 34-35; Donald Miralle / Allsport; p. 37; Ezra Shaw; p. 40; Tom Hauck / Allsport; p. 41, Tom Hauck / Allsport; p. 42, Ezra Shaw / Allsport; p. 44, Ezra Shaw; p. 46, Ezra Shaw; p. 48; Ezra Shaw.

Library of Congress Cataloging-in-Publication Data is available.

ISBN 0-448-42552-1 (pbk) A B C D E F G H I J

ALL
ABOARD
READING™

Level 3
Grades 2-3

Shaquille O'Neal
Man of Steel

By Douglas Bradshaw

Grosset & Dunlap • New York

Super Shaq

The date is March 6, 2000. The Los Angeles Lakers are playing their crosstown rival, the L.A. Clippers. Number 34 pushes and shoves his way into position. A defender tries to stop him but can't—and for good reason. Number 34 is too big and too strong. He stands 7 feet 1 inch tall and weighs 320 pounds. He wears a size 22 shoe. Tattooed on his left arm are the Superman "S" and the words "Man of Steel." He puts his hand in the air and calls for the basketball. He gets it. And in one smooth move, he turns and slams the ball into the basket. He plays his position, center, like no one else in the league.

Who is Number 34?

Shaquille O'Neal, that's who.

Today is Shaq's twenty-eighth birthday
and he wants to make it special. By the
end of the first half, the Lakers are
winning 56–55. Shaq has already scored
26 points. But what he's aiming for
tonight is fifty. He continues to run the

floor, and by the end of the third quarter, Shaq has 42 points. Almost there!

In the fourth quarter, Shaq throws down a huge slam, breaking his old record of 53 points. The crowd goes crazy. With 5:25 left, the Lakers are winning, so Shaq listens to the fans and tries for 60. And with just 3:24 left in the game, Shaq slams home his sixty–first point. He is the first Laker since 1969 to score 60 points in a game. Satisfied, he sits down on the bench. The entire stadium chants "MVP! MVP!" then sings "Happy Birthday" to him. Shaquille O'Neal certainly has given himself a great birthday present.

He makes playing basketball look *so* easy. But it's not, even for Shaq. He has worked hard for years to become basketball's Man of Steel.

Growing Up, Up and Away

Shaquille Rashaun O'Neal was born in a poor part of Newark, New Jersey, on March 6, 1972. The name Shaquille Rashaun is Islamic. It means "little warrior." Shaq, the oldest of four children, has two sisters, LaTeefah and Ayesha, and one brother named Jamal.

When Shaq was just a baby, Philip Harrison married Shaq's mother, Lucille O'Neal. Harrison wanted to give them a better life, so he joined the U.S. Army and became a drill sergeant. Shaq's dad was strict, but fair. He taught Shaq and his brother and sisters many lessons. One

Shaq enjoying a Laker win with his mom

of the most important lessons was that "the world has too many followers." He told them to be a leader. The guys hanging out on the corner, selling drugs, and getting into trouble were followers. Shaq has said that had it not been for his father, "I'd be a troublemaker on the street."

As a child, Shaq lived in many different places. Because his father was in the Army, Shaq and the family often moved from base to base. This meant that Shaq kept leaving old friends and having to make new ones. During his childhood, he moved from New Jersey to Georgia to Germany to Texas. He was always the new kid in school. Because Shaq was so big, he stuck out like a sore thumb.

Shaq was embarrassed by his size. He just wanted to look like everyone else. But he didn't—he was supersized! When Shaq was eight years old, he was 4 feet 9 inches tall. At ten, he was 5 feet 3 inches tall. And by age thirteen, Shaq was 6 feet 8 inches tall! He wore a size 17 shoe. That's about fifteen inches long! To make things worse, he was clumsy. He played football, baseball, and basketball, but he

Shaq shows off his oversized sneaker to a young fan

wasn't very good at any of them. The
other kids teased him. Shaq thought that
if he could make his classmates laugh,
they would like him. So, he became the
class clown. It was Shaq's way of fitting in.

While living on an Army base in
Germany, Shaq took part in a basketball
camp. It was run by a coach named Dale
Brown. Brown was the head coach of the
Louisiana State University (LSU) Tigers.

Shaq asked Coach Brown how he could become a stronger player, "because I'm 6 feet 8 inches and I can't jump." Coach Brown asked, "What rank are you, soldier?" Shaq told him he wasn't in the Army—he was only thirteen years old!

Former LSU head coach Dale Brown

Coach Brown was amazed at the boy's size. He realized that with the proper training, one day Shaq might be a basketball superstar. The coach asked to speak with Shaq's father. He wanted the family to consider sending Shaq to LSU when he was old enough for college. Shaq's dad said he would consider it—but only if Shaq got a good education and didn't just play basketball. Coach Brown gave his word on that. And for the next four years, Shaq and Coach Brown were pen pals.

As Shaq grew older, basketball became more and more important to him. His childhood hero was Julius "Dr. J" Erving, the Philadelphia 76ers superstar. Still, Shaq's first loves were music and dancing. Young Shaq wanted to be a TV star. He loved to break dance. Shaq could even spin on his head! But he continued to grow and grow. And by the time he was fourteen years old, Shaq decided that he should start to focus on something that his body was naturally suited for—basketball.

So Shaq began working harder on his basketball skills. Even so, he was cut from his ninth-grade team. The coach said that Shaq was too clumsy and that his big feet got in the way. Shaq was very disappointed, but he didn't give up. Instead, he worked harder. He focused on both basketball *and* schoolwork. Shaq wanted to be a leader. He wanted to be the best. His dream was to play in the National Basketball Association (NBA) and to win the championship.

In the spring of 1987, the family moved to San Antonio, Texas. Shaq, now fifteen years old, enrolled at Robert G. Cole Senior High School. He continued to study hard and practice basketball every day. Finally, all the hard work started to pay off. Not only did Shaq make the basketball team, but he was the starting center. And during his junior and senior years, Shaq led the Cole basketball team to a 68–1 record.

Shaquille O'Neal at Robert G. Cole High School

There were still bad days. What Shaq has called "the worst moment of my life" happened during a game in eleventh grade. Shaq committed four fouls in the first two minutes. He was benched for almost the entire game, but went back in as the clock ticked down. Shaq's team was behind by one point. There were only ten seconds left. Then, Shaq was fouled. He had to shoot two free throws. If he made the free throws, his team would win and go to the state finals.

Shaq missed them both.

Shaq took the loss hard. He felt terrible for weeks. He had let his team down. Shaq's father told him, "Don't worry about it. Work on your free throws, come back and win the championship next year." He did just that. The next year, Shaq led his team to a victory in the state championship.

Over his two years at Cole Senior High School, he averaged 32 points, 22 rebounds and 8 blocked shots per game. Shaq had become one of the top high school players in the country.

The Shaq Attack—Rising Superstar

The time had come for Shaq to decide on college. He chose to attend LSU and play basketball for his longtime friend, Coach Brown. But once again, things were not easy. He missed his family. It was the first time he had ever been away from them.

Also, college basketball was much tougher than high school basketball. Opposing coaches would set up plays to stop Shaq. Sometimes, he was double- or even triple-teamed! So Shaq learned to pass quickly, shoot a jumper, and put up a hook shot. He practiced and practiced.

Soon, Shaq was unstoppable. He was no longer a clumsy kid embarrassed by his size. He was now a terrific athlete. For two years in a row, Shaq was named a first team All-American. That meant that he was one of the very best college basketball players in the U.S.

In 1992, Shaq entered the National Basketball Association's college draft. This is how professional teams pick college or high school basketball players to play for them. Each pro team is given one pick in each of the draft's two 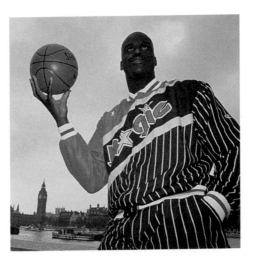 rounds. The Orlando Magic had the very first draft pick. The Magic's owner, general manager, and the coach all wanted the same player. They selected Shaquille O'Neal! Shaq had made it to the NBA! The first part of his dream had come true.

Once Shaq got to Orlando, he quickly impressed the coaches with his good attitude. In his first few games for the Magic, Shaq played so well that he was named NBA Player of the Week. That year, he was voted to start in the All-Star Game—the first rookie to do so since Michael Jordan in 1985! And it came as no surprise that he was also named the NBA Rookie of the Year. With Shaq leading the way, the Magic won twenty games more than they had the year before. Shaq was an instant superstar.

But Shaq never gave up his childhood love of music and dancing. With his newfound celebrity, he started making rap and hip-hop albums and music videos. He released his first album, *Shaq Diesel*, in 1993. It didn't stop there. He acted in movies and even made a Shaq video game!

Now if he could snare a championship for the Orlando Magic, he would be on top of the world. But in the 1993–94 season, Shaq did not get past the first round of the playoffs. The Magic were swept by the Indiana Pacers.

In 1994–95, Shaq led the Magic all the way to the NBA Finals. But the Finals were a nightmare. The Houston Rockets crushed the Magic in four games. Again, there would be no championship.

After working hard in the off-season, Shaq hoped that the 1995–96 season was going to be different. He thought that his team could win it all. But on October 24, in a preseason game against the Miami Heat, Shaq made a move for the basket. Heat center Matt Geiger tried to stop him and chopped at Shaq's hand. Hard. Shaq left the game with a broken thumb, and had surgery two days later. Shaq was angry and frustrated. This wasn't the first time he had been banged up. Shaq felt that sometimes players who couldn't stop him tried to hurt him.

Shaq tried not to let his injury get him down. He missed the first third of the season but came roaring back. Once again he led the Magic to the playoffs . . . and once again they got swept—this time by the Chicago Bulls. It was the third straight time Shaq and the Magic had been crushed 4–0 in a playoff series. It

Shaq tries to stop Chicago Bulls superstar, Michael Jordan

seemed as if they couldn't win when it counted most.

Shaq's contract with Orlando ended after the 1995–96 season. Shaq was now a free agent. That meant that *he* could pick the NBA team he would play for—as long as that team wanted him. And, of course, *everybody* wanted Shaq. He had some difficult decisions to make. The Magic

The 1999-2000 Lakers basketball team

wanted Shaq to stay, but he wondered if they were a good enough team to get back to the Finals, and more importantly, to win.

In the end, he decided to make a move. He signed with the Los Angeles Lakers. It would be a new start with a fresh, young team. The Lakers were full of talent, but they hadn't won a championship since 1988. They needed a great big man. It

seemed like a perfect match. Shaq said, "It was the best offer because of the players surrounding me, the staff, and the organization."

Shaq was excited to wear the legendary Laker purple and gold. He wanted to clinch a championship for the team that had won five of them in the 1980s.

1996 was a very special year for Shaq. He was named one of the fifty greatest players of all time and selected to be part of the USA Olympic basketball team, known as "Dream Team II." They won the gold medal at the Olympics in Atlanta. Shaq felt proud when he received his gold medal, but he never forgot what he wanted even more—an NBA championship ring.

Building an NBA championship team is like putting together a jigsaw puzzle.

Shaq at the 1996 Olympic games

All the pieces have to fit. Shaq knew that
a team needs at least two great players at
its "heart." In the 1980s he had watched
Magic Johnson and Kareem Abdul-Jabar
with the Lakers. In the 1990s he had
watched Michael Jordan and Scottie

Pippen with the Chicago Bulls. Shaq knew he could be part of another great duo. And he thought that Kobe Bryant, the Lakers' extremely talented eighteen-year-old rookie, could be the other half. Kobe was an exciting and explosive guard. If they could learn to work together, they could be the heart of the next great team. But Kobe was young. He was going to need time.

Shaq was willing to wait. He was happy about moving to Los Angeles. He loved the fans, and he loved being part of a team with such a great history. And living so close to Hollywood allowed Shaq to continue his singing and acting careers. More albums, TV appearances, and movies followed, including the starring role in the movie *Steel*—the story of a crime-fighting superhero who wears a suit of steel.

Shaq was famous and Shaq was rich, yet he never forgot the poor streets where he

Kobe Bryant guards Jason Kidd as Shaq stands by

came from. He gave both his time and money to children's charities. Shaq donated one million dollars to the Boys & Girls Clubs of America. The money was used to set up computer centers all over the U.S. where kids could learn to use the Internet. At Christmas, Shaq would dress up as "Shaq-a-Claus," and give toys away to needy children. Thanksgiving became "Shaqsgiving," with Shaq himself serving dinner to hundreds of poor families. At Easter, Shaq dressed up as the biggest Easter bunny of all time.

In many ways, Shaq *was* a Superman, coming to the aid of people in need. But in other ways, Shaq was only human. His injuries were proof of that. Shaq kept getting hurt. In 1996–97, he had to sit out 28 games with a knee injury. He missed 20 games in 1997–98 due to a broken wrist and pulled muscles in his stomach that took a year to heal! Because of injury, Shaq didn't feel he played his best during the whole 1998–99 season. In frustration, Shaq said, "It's never going to heal. I'm going to have this problem for the rest of my life." Like a true warrior, Shaq fought through the injuries and the pain.

Still, each year the Lakers would make it to the playoffs and be eliminated early. It was just like back at Orlando. Again Shaq started wondering if he would get to wear an NBA championship ring. What was the problem? What was missing?

Super Year

Although Shaq and Kobe had indeed become the "heart" of the Lakers, something was still missing. The Lakers still weren't a "great team." The piece that was missing was a top-notch coach. But, in 1999, the Lakers found coach Phil Jackson. Jackson had coached the great Michael Jordan and the mighty Chicago Bulls to six NBA championships in the 1990s. He now came on board as the Lakers head coach. Jackson was strict, but fair—like Shaq's dad. Shaq admired that in a coach. Shaq knew this was the start of something great.

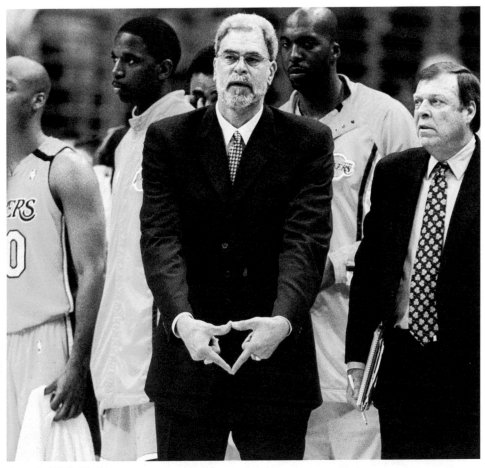

Coach Phil Jackson

Right away Jackson had the respect of the team. Along with his NBA championship rings, Jackson brought a deep understanding of the game. He wasn't afraid to shake things up. He told Shaq that he had to give up two things. The first was twenty pounds. (Shaq now weighed almost 350 pounds!) The second was some of his scoring. Jackson wanted Shaq to work on his defense as well as his offense. He wanted Shaq to become a better all-around player—that meant shot blocking, rebounding, and field-goal accuracy. Jackson said that these changes

would help the team. Shaq agreed. Coach Jackson also made it clear to everybody that this was "Shaq's team." Shaq was the leader on the court. He agreed with that, too!

With Jackson coaching the 1999–2000 Lakers, the players had a new attitude.

They *knew* they were the best. Even when they fell behind in a game, they never worried. They continued to play hard and usually won. During the season, the Lakers went on winning streaks of both 23–1 and 30–1. Shaq was unstoppable. He scored and rebounded and scored some more. The Lakers finished the regular season with the best record in basketball, 67–15.

Shaq liked Coach Jackson's fast-paced game plan. It kept the players running and on their toes. Called the triangle offense, it meant that Shaq would get the ball almost every time down the court. If Shaq had a shot, he would take it. If he didn't, he would make a quick pass to a teammate. "Good things open up when everyone's moving," Shaq said, "It's like we have twenty different plays inside one."

Shaq and Kobe played like Jackson's

Kobe makes a quick pass to Shaq

triangle offense had been made just for them. They became the most exciting combination in the NBA. At times, it seemed like they were reading each other's minds . . . Many times, a game would be on the line. The Lakers would need a basket. Then, Kobe would throw up a perfect alley-oop. Shaq would reach high into the air and slamdunk the ball for a score. The Lakers' fans would go wild. With Shaq and Kobe in "the zone," other teams never stood a chance!

The 1999–2000 season was huge for Shaq. He won the scoring title and was named the All-Star Game MVP and the regular season MVP! He was on top of the NBA. All the awards made Shaq feel very happy and proud. But he was still waiting for the one thing he wanted more than anything else—an NBA championship.

Champions at Last—
Superman Gets His Ring

The Lakers had fought their way
through the first two rounds of the
playoffs, beating the Sacramento Kings
and the Phoenix Suns. Then they met up
with the Portland Trail Blazers in the
Western Conference Finals. The series
was a battle. The Trail Blazers pushed it
to Game 7. The winner would go to the
Finals, and the loser would go home.

By the third quarter of Game 7, it
didn't look good for the Lakers. Kobe was
limping around on a sprained ankle. The
team was down by 16 points. But Coach

Jackson kept his players calm and no one gave up. They battled back. With just a couple minutes remaining, Shaq and Kobe saw an opportunity for their signature play. Kobe threw up an alley-oop that only a superman could reach. Shaq leaped, soared into the air, and smashed the ball through the hoop!

Super Shaq grabs an alley-oop and slams the ball

The fans went crazy. The Lakers had beaten Portland 89-84. Now it was on to the NBA Finals against the Indiana Pacers.

The Pacers were led by superstar Reggie Miller and their own big man, 7 foot 4 inch Rik Smits. The Pacers had another superstar on the bench—Coach Larry Bird. He was one of the greatest ever to play the game.

The Lakers won the first two games. Shaq turned into a superman. He totaled 83 points and 43 rebounds. Smits could do nothing against Shaq on either end of the floor. The

Former Indiana Coach Larry Bird

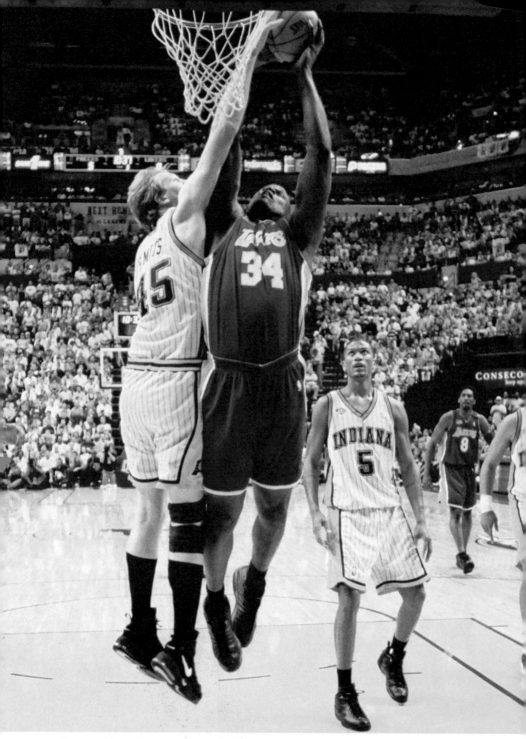

Shaq and Pacer Rik Smits go for a rebound

Pacers were in big trouble. But Game 3 was back on their home court in Indiana. The Pacer fans helped their team rally and pull out a 100–91 win. Shaq, who scored 33 points but made only 3 of 13 foul shots, was upset with the way the Lakers played. He said, "the Pacers just wanted it more. They just played a little harder."

In Game 4, the Lakers came back. Shaq poured in 36 points, grabbed 21 rebounds, and powered the Lakers past the Pacers in overtime. Was Indiana finished? They were down 3–1, but Bird and the Pacers did not give up. They came back and crushed the Lakers, 120–87, in Game 5. Could the Pacers come back to win the series? Would Shaq and the Lakers choke?

Game 6 was back in L.A. The Pacers

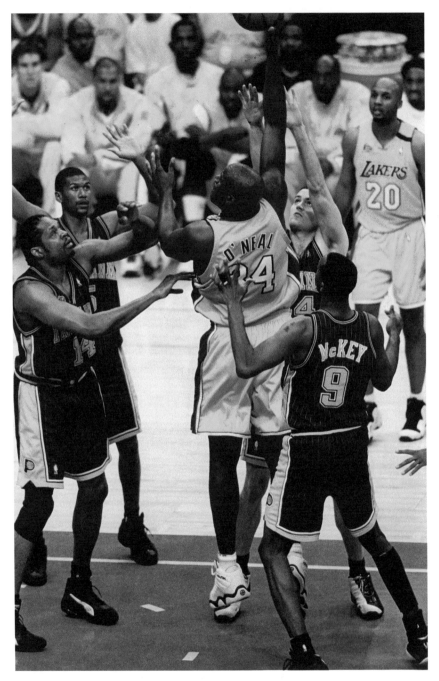

Shaq shoots the ball as the Lakers bench looks on

again came out strong and led through most of the game. But Shaq kept it close. He had 15 of the Lakers' first 29 points. He wanted the championship, and he wanted it tonight. The Pacers had other ideas. They led by as many as 12 points in the second quarter. But with less than six minutes remaining in the third quarter, the Lakers were able to cut the lead to one point. From then on, the game was up for grabs!

With only a couple minutes left in the game, the Lakers tried to pull away. Then Miller hit a big three-pointer. Still, Shaq refused to crumble. He pulled his teammates together and said, "Let's just get this done." And they did. Shaq had come up big. He scored 41 points, 13 in the fourth quarter, and grabbed 12 rebounds. With 2.5 seconds left, Kobe hit

his last two foul shots to finish off the
Pacers, 116–111.

Shaq and the Lakers had done it!
They were world champions! Shaq and
Kobe hugged each other on the court.
Big Shaq cried as purple and gold

confetti rained down around them. "I think they were just tears of joy," Shaq said. "Eight long years of failing . . . so all that stuff just came out."

Shaq finally had his championship. He *was* the best. He became only the third player in NBA history to win the regular season MVP, All-Star Game MVP, and the Finals MVP, all in the same year.

As the crowd cheered, Shaq ran over to his family and hugged his mother. She told him how happy she was for him. But where was Shaq's father? He wasn't even in L.A. He had stayed at home in Orlando. The tough drill sergeant was afraid he would get too emotional if he went to his son's game.

When asked about his championship ring, Shaq said, "When I get the ring, I'm just going to look at it, then I'm going to give it to my father." Without his father's lessons of leadership, would Shaq be where he is today? Shaq doesn't think so. "The first one is for you daddy," he said. But the next ring, Shaq said, "the next one will be mine." And chances are good there *will be* a next one, for Shaquille O'Neal—Man of Steel.